# The Thing Itself

# The Thing Itself

### Poems
### Terry Lucas

### Photographs
### Gary Topper

Longship Press     San Rafael, California

Copyright © 2020 by Terry Lucas and Gary Topper
All Rights Reserved

Published in the United States by Longship Press, San Rafael, California.
Neither the whole nor part of this book may be copied, reproduced, scanned or otherwise duplicated or distributed without the written consent of the publisher.

For more information, go to www.longshippress.com.
Inquiries about the poems or photographs may be directed to
Lawrence Tjernell, Editor
Longship Press (info@longshippress.com).

ISBN-13:
978-0-578-78583-7

L O N G S H I P  P R E S S

Longship Press

Printed in the United States
All American Printing Services, Petaluma, CA

Longship Press 1122 4th Street San Rafael, California 94901

*Not Ideas About the Thing But the Thing Itself*

— Wallace Stevens

## List of Poems

| | |
|---|---|
| By Any Other Name | 2 |
| Safeway | 5 |
| The Arrival | 6 |
| When She's Gone | 8 |
| Shiprock | 11 |
| The Thing Itself (A Cento) | 12 |
| Morning Ritual | 16 |
| New Mexico Sighting | 19 |
| Dharma Rain | 20 |
| Spirit | 25 |
| Infinity | 26 |
| Recycling | 28 |
| Neighbors At 2 A.M. | 32 |
| Sleep | 34 |
| To the Fog | 36 |
| Vortices | 39 |
| Good House Hunting | 40 |
| I never wanted to be a poet | 42 |
| Parrots | 46 |
| Dear Frogs of Pinckneyville, Illinois | 48 |
| Chicken | 51 |
| Return of the Purple Martins | 52 |
| Horse Latitudes | 54 |
| Returning To My Childhood Home Thirty Years After Foreclosure | 58 |
| First Love | 62 |
| Easy | 65 |
| Starbucks took you away: my barista, my double | 66 |
| A Small Pebble | 68 |
| Slow Dancing | 70 |
| All roads | 72 |

## By Any Other Name

*August 2006*

They voted Pluto off the list of planets,
one less note in the music of the spheres.
News of this reaches me too late to show up

for the debate and argue for snowball
dwarfs, diminution, and eccentric orbs
cutting through the plane of Neptune — instead

I will write this missive and read the annual
reports which I predict will change as bodies
wobble their way in and out of favor. Also,

I will listen to the sound of my Apple
laptop instead of my manual Remington
cutting into twenty-pound paper, ink

filling in depressions and gashes on
scrolled pages. What isn't history? Or
for that matter, this story of changing

names and places, written in fading script,
harvested from cuttlefish, octopi, and squid
killed in the midst of sepia clouds,

bodies luminescent after death — yes
there are nights you could read by the light
cast upon Pluto by its full moon, Styx.

# Safeway

I love my grocery store. I love to roam
its aisles — Keebler Elves, the Jolly Green Giant

shuffling for position with jellied Spam,
frozen pizza plastered with pepperoni

discs ready to fly down my throat, hover
in my stomach, disembark its fat

little passengers to march straight to my heart.
The floral department's sign reads *Poetry*

*in Bloom* above papery black edges of roses red
and violets blue. You can have your Trader Joe's,

your Whole Foods, your Non-GMO, gluten-free,
organic-only Good Earth. I want a real grocery store

with hormones in the beef, pharmacy attached, pain
killers within arm's reach of a packaged heart attack.

My Safeway makes me feel safe. Come the apocalypse
I'll be trapped inside, popping OXY, singing in the singularity

techies say is coming, thawing out a T-bone
on a Weber grill, drinking a ten dollar bottle of pinot,

staring out the window for signs of life,
of death. Pretty much doing what I do now at home.

## The Arrival

*28 December 1895*

Two platforms give
Perspective to the opening

Silent scene from *The Arrival
Of a Train at La Ciotat Station*.

Orthogonals merge, tweezing a
Smoldering dot, growing wheels,

Smokestack, bell — & now the tail
Emerges from the vanishing point, in

Full view of the crowd gathered in the
Grand Café's basement, watching the black

Boiler bulge, fill the screen on the wall with soot
& steam, threatening to burst through studs into the

Dining room, break vases of chrysanthemums, plates
Of half-eaten Crepes Flambé — waiters scattering, cutting

Through the flickering, dust-flecked beams of light — never
Shining again with such surprise, such innocence, such living black & white.

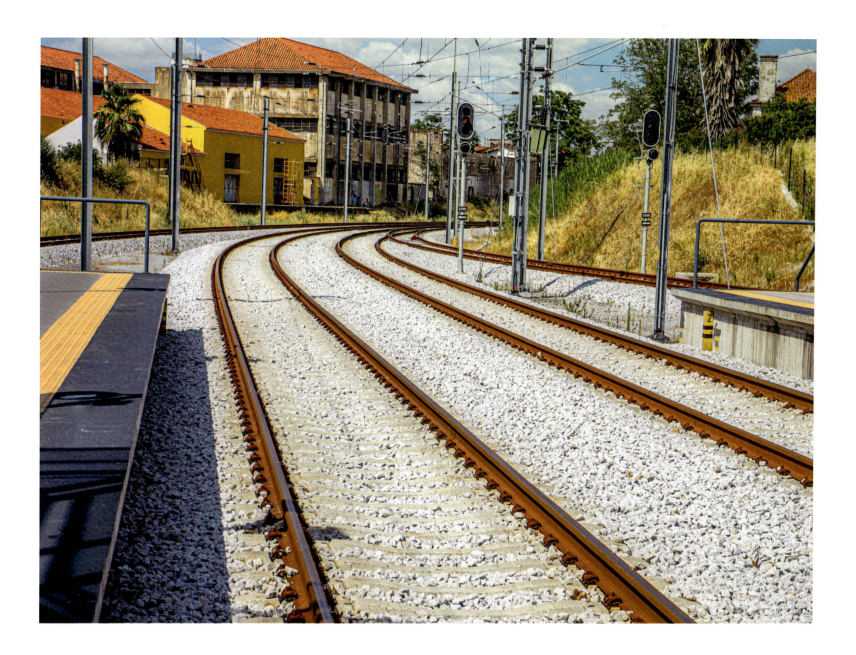

## When She's Gone

On the Brown Line again to the city,
windows lined up like LCD TVs

on the weather channel — gray frozen limbs
making their entrance stage left, history

screeching on the other side of the aisle
from the right. No matter, the car is rocking

all of us down the same tracks, the tanned moon
is dancing through trees in her clouded gown,

conniving to leave us for another
lover. And there is nothing we can do

except watch her — she pulls one shoulder a-
way, unraveling Earth's hold on her waist —

how she glides toward the brilliant dark doorway —

how we will tilt on our side when she's gone.

# Shiprock

> *Tsé Bit'a'í*

Cutting your way through dust storms, waves
Of sand blow over your prow, settle on foils of stone,
Wash down the ribs of your hull to crystal sea.

> *The Navajos say you sailed from the north,*
> *A great bird saving their people from the flood,*
> *Crashing into the desert, burying all*
> *But your wings and tail: sole cremains of salvation.*

What is it that makes a man or woman
Set out on foot for you? Your jagged masts that reach
For gibbous moon? Ancient lens of atmosphere?

> *The old ones still believe the blood*
> *Will return to petrified feathers,*
> *Carry them away when the flood returns.*

Grasses and sedges with no names, abandoned
Frames of cars and trucks, a valley of dried bones
That will never rest, never rise again?

> *Shiprock! Cry out from beneath the desert;*
> *Call your brothers and sisters from the flood.*

The overwhelming flood of sand
Is all that will mark their graves.

> *Sand enough to stem the flood.*

## The Thing Itself (A Cento)

You know how hard it is sometimes just to walk on the streets
Downtown, how everything enters you —
Iron straight from the forge, fierce with tiny agitation,
Rain ringing like teeth in the beggar's tin,
Like a sinking ship drowning its lights,
Chalk beds    trilobites      giant ferns
Whirr. The invisible sponsored again by white
Isotopes, pockets, dragonflies, bread:
There is no dictionary for this gathering.
You might think you were Noah
Failing to arrange a taxonomy of allergic substances.
Our lives are like birds' lives, flying around, blown away,
Or some far horn repeating over water —
Do we simply join our arcs
The way a seed is pressed into a hole?
Don't ask me any questions, I've seen how things
Blink-quick, or quicker still,
Tracked under the brown fog of a winter dawn,
Follow the light, the twist and drop of blackbirds from the tree.

## Morning Ritual

In the mirror I inventory spots and lumps
on my mostly denuded body, assessing

any change in color or size. I visualize
eight million years of hair loss, ancestors

once semi-aquatic later suffering heat stroke,
perhaps irritating parasitic beginnings

of malaria or Lyme disease as they moved
out of the African savanna.

My triple-bladed razor excises traces
of hirsute lineage from my space-time face.

Safely tucked beneath hair and bone,
mitochondria in my brain rehearse

their workday full of meetings to decide
which cells live, which die, what diseases

will be revealed on the epidermis before
our star swells to the size of Mars' orbit,

before blood and bumps boil away —
before tonight's bottle of Beaujolais.

## New Mexico Sighting

*Melanistic Canis Latrans*

A wild dog, we thought, at least partly
fed by Navajos — erect body shining
like a seal's, soaked with the afternoon
sun — all we could make of your gaze
at two hundred yards. But when you turned,
silhouetting your muzzle, loping into the desert,
your tail swaying like a juniper bush,
as much at home among the sage
as sage itself, we knew you were not
tracking hogans painted on horizon. Descending
the plutonic spine that percolated up through this plateau
twenty-six million years ago, we lost
sight of you, but still whispered as if you were the trickster
god we didn't want to wake, the dream
we didn't want to leave, longing for
one more glimpse, somehow
to confirm your presence, your mystery — and ours.

## Dharma Rain

> *In the summer of 2008, when wildfire descended on Tassajara Zen Center, the oldest Zen monastery outside Asia, The Forest Service evacuated all residents. Five monks turned back and met the fire, saving Tassajara.*
>
> — Adapted from *Fire Monks: Zen Mind Meets Wildfire at the Gates of Tassajara*

It was Dharma Rain
    met you, Dharma Rain
from granite wine

    pumped from the creek
through PVC pipe
    soaking wooden buildings,

dirt, stone, skin —
    sprinklers the sound
of sustained violins —

    strings creating their own
sultry atmosphere —
    your fiery, brass choir

waiting for the director's baton
    to cue you in. It was the Fire
Monk Jazz Quintet

    rearranged the score,
re-harmonized the minor-chord flame-song,
    Jump, Jive, An' Wailin'

fire-hose saxophones
        swingin' with your drivin'
hot-rock rhythms

        and log-rollin' bass notes,
cascading down into the smoke-
        filled gulch,

the whole valley smelling
        like the world's original singe —
you, up on the ridge,

        ripping off red blouses
from manzanitas and madrones,
        becoming more aroused

with each naked limb, each torso
        exposed in firelight.
You crowned them one-by-one,

        but couldn't penetrate
the V-shaped ravine, though you tried
        like a wedding-night groom

but in the end, more out of duty
        than desire, you stumbled drunk
into the bed

        of the garden, soft
glow buried in her
        loam, her mist.

*Conceived of flash*
       *between earth and sky,*
*I smoldered three days*

       *beneath dust. Born hungry*
*for live oak, sycamore,*
       *maple — compelled to carve*

*paths through the chaparral —*
       *maroon-barked manzanita,*
*chamise, ceanothus, yucca —*

       *to enlighten all flesh*
*in my oven mouth —*
       *in one breath*

*to translate a trillion tree lines,*
       *a billion pages of bay laurel*
*into fire beetles and whispering bells.*

       *O Tassajara,*
*when your lanterns were lit*
       *along the engawa*

*surrounding your zendo*
       *this morning, I saw you —*
*the frost of your skin, your body,*

       *your vulnerable ground,*
*fire monk boots making little Buddha-shapes*
       *in the wet dirt.*

*I saw your treetops aligned*
    *like piano keys,*
*each taut string*

    *tied to nothingness, waiting*
*for my vermilion finger*
    *-nailed touch.*

*Then I turned*
    *to the moist commerce*
*of your temple gate and yurts,*

    *chemical-filled sheds,*
*pine rooms and cabins,*
    *birdhouse and pool,*

*your schist stone Buddha,*
    *eyes brushed closed,*
*buried in the bocce ball court,*

    *calling down my parched tongues*
*to lap your Dharma Rain, your granite wine,*
    *to suckle the icicle of you.*

# Spirit

*After Campbell McGrath*

We construct it from water and motion and breath,
      smoke, tremors, tongues
      of fire, desire to live between
the growing distances of the stars.

It is, for all its freedom and aspiration,
      an artifact of human agency —
      the universe become conscious,
poured into cracked urns of flesh.

Its insistent voice mirrored by a hungry ear,
      like the lesser light that rules the night
      reflecting the ancient of days. Old
as the odor of resin-soaked wood on the pyre,

dancing to blood-orange flames,
      fashioned from the atmosphere,
      dark matter, energy, air,
shaped and assembled deed by deed,

and finished with feathers of ice.
      We build it on a loom that turns
      straw thoughts into golden bullion,
then lock it in its chest and hope it can save us.

## Infinity

If infinity
really exists,

that compact package
the big bang came in

contains more than everything —
precisely one more present than the last,

and then one more forever, all wrapped in ribbons
of Mobius strips. If infinity really exists, every day turns out

to be lightning's birthday. Each flash of every blown-out second,
a train emerges from inside a twisted tunnel, where the tracks

have crossed without derailing cars, carrying passengers
dressed in coats and hats like ours, staring at our faces

in the windows, not a single hair on their heads
uncloned, each unbrushed thought falling

wildly into place, each whorled
fingertip on each cold

pane of glass —
a kiss.

## Recycling

I am wheeling the recycling bin
down the driveway, the steep
pot-holed driveway, eighteen percent
grade, making it impossible
for trucks to negotiate
up through freighted foliage to our house.
I am thinking about the plastic Arrowhead
water bottles, broken down
cardboard boxes, Ball Mason jars
with a faint grape odor
I am sending out into the world,
after having consumed their contents —
I am wondering where they will go,
if I will see them again, and if I would
recognize them in another form
or universe.
              I am wondering about the day
the wood pulp in the cardboard was conceived
from a single photon of sunlight striking
one green leaf of perhaps the great-
great-grandmother of this eucalyptus tree
or that balsam fir. And I am amazed at the thought
of breathing in molecules of air,
exhaled from plants, as well as from people
dead for years: Darwin, Shakespeare,
Whitman, Crane swirling in my lungs —
their embered words, unreadable
heat signatures, along with the last breath

sucked from the chest of some rapist
on death row, a thief
hanging on a cross by nails
fashioned from iron smelted in a star
gone nova over five billion years ago —
the same metal hammering through my veins,
straining to drudge more
oxygen to my legs as I walk
back up the crumbling asphalt,
loose gravel anting toward the ocean — mother
ocean stretching as tall as she can with every wave
for a glimpse of her prodigal children returning home.

## Neighbors At 2 A.M.

They're fighting again. Shouting and throwing
clothes off their balcony, several stories
above us — billowing silk blouses, distressed
jeans — flailing half-human forms plunging
toward cool sod like suicides. One by one,
lights are coming on in the courtyard of the complex.
A humid night, gray-green fog has gathered
in damp St. Augustine, like the angel of death
in Cecil B. DeMille's *The Ten Commandments*.
Shouldn't we smear blood on our doorposts,
our lintels? Blood — isn't that what *they* are after,
turning themselves inside out, drowning
each other in the rapids of their hearts,
getting swept over the falls, swearing a final oath
in Oblivion's bittersweet name? Shouldn't we all
gather at the river, tread its bright banks,
find a sacred spot where laurels exhale their long, unison breath —
every leaf a tongue, every branch a choir
canting its last overture? Don't we need
to sit zazen in the midst of gnarled trunks,
offer confessions? Listen — now the sound
of furniture breaking on the rocks below
our window, a surfeit of hate shaking
our foundation — flecks of spackle sifting
through the tired light of our own closets,
like sequins falling from a wedding gown.

# Sleep

*After Kim Addonizio*

*You know how hard it is sometimes*
when your half of the world is passing
through shadow, calling to you
to join it, because darkness always wants more
darkness, even though you're tossing inside
your own inky dust, signals from home lost
as if you were an astronaut on the far side of the moon,
waiting for earth's blue marble to reappear —
you can't sleep, you can't

escape memory's ancient terrain spooling through
your brain, impact craters from heavenly bodies
slamming again and again into your feverish skin,
while you're straining to hear the words
that will tell you when to shut down
your burn, but all that rises from your pillow
is the scratch of static, all you can do is rehearse
your re-entry, your splashdown
into morning's gray waves.                    Your re-entry,
your splashdown into morning's gray waves
is all you can do to rehearse the burn, the scratch
of static rising from your pillow telling you
to shut down, while you strain to hear
the words slamming again and again
into the feverish skin of your brain —
impact craters from heavenly bodies,
memory's ancient terrain spooling
toward sleep — but you can't
wait for earth's blue marble to re-appear,
as if you were an astronaut on the far side
of the moon's inky dust, signals lost
while you are tossing inside
darkness, because darkness always wants more
shadow, calling to you
when your half of the world is passing —
*you know how hard it is sometimes.*

## To the Fog

And then you wake up one morning to the fog
Surrounding your house like a heaven,
Like the first time you drank a whole bottle
Of white wine alone. You get dressed for your walk
Down the path you walk on each day.
You look to the horizon, the shouting
Sun now more like moon's soft hum. One muted tone
Behind sky's veil. You notice the lichen-
Covered stones greeting each step, the geometry
Of downed limbs scratching at low tide,
The snowy egret you surprise, plumed head
Turned on its side, sweeping the mudflats, improvising
A way to catch breakfast in suffused light —
All of this and more, normally hidden in plain sight.
But an orchestra's warming up behind the curtain:
Commuters leaning on shrill horns, distant
Sirens rising, the engines of this world
Revving up their clear intent to perform
Something short of a miracle. O fog
Of morning, hover in the hollows of this day,
Remain in its low places, to rise up again
When we need not more, but less.

## Vortices

We all eventually stumble into our own story.
Every big bang has an infinite number
Of smaller bangs struggling to get out.
For our purposes there are no other purposes.
Theoretically the atoms in you left foot came from a star
Different from the one that donated its atoms to your right.
Some theories are full of theorists.
And some holes are full of stories.
Black ones with event horizons big enough to hold
All the lines ever written in the universe.
But that's another story.
Watch your step.

## Good House Hunting

*1974*

New Year's Day, after driving all night
across two states, my wife and I, sated

with full stacks of buckwheat pancakes, sausage,
and gravy, are seated in a red vinyl booth

at an IHOP on Seminary Drive in south Fort Worth.
A *Star-Telegram* classified section is spread

across the Formica table etched with atomic pattern,
next to an unfolded city map. We scan

butter-smudged newsprint with syrup-sticky fingertips,
as only twenty-four-year-olds can — a rolled-up life

savings of five hundred dollars stashed in my low-rise
bell-bottom jeans pocket. Both of us are flush

with faith the next listing in the "for rent" column
will be the house we've been stalking —

affordable, close to school and work,
so our Mazda will burn less gas.

I once read about a Yellow Warbler named Wally
(leg band #1750), that returned to mate for most

of a decade at the same spot in Ontario.
He traveled twice the Earth's circumference,

and fathered forty fledglings that likewise returned
annually to the family nest. I learned only half

of all songbirds live past one season,
that many fly with intent

at windows, car mirrors, and hubcaps,
fending off brazen intruders — their own

reflections. And mockingbirds have been known
to imitate car alarms, subway trains, blending in

with their surroundings. No longer do I
list Southwestern Seminary on my resume,

live in Fort Worth, or even in Texas. I left
the woman with whom I shared the house

we found that day. And now my faith
is in the *Imago Dei* I see in a sunrise

over the New Mexican Sangre de Cristos —
a reflection of me, no longer caring to be camouflaged,

returning home on crimson wings.

## I never wanted to be a poet

before we moved into that converted gas station
on the outskirts of Deming, where dust storms gave up
their ghosts to the shapes of cars and trucks —
one minute nothing out our window but brown
canvas, the next a traveler drawn in
beside the lifeless pumps, staggering toward our door,
screams and slaps cutting through sand's static
as the office sign swung against stucco facade.
But something else, one of us said, did you hear
the sound of a trapped animal crying for us
to open up goddammit and give them some gas
to make it out of this hellhole? Once,
when you were alone and naked, standing
in the grease pit that was now our living room,
a man walked in on you because I'd failed
to lock the door. Later, when you told me the story,
you yelled for the first time in our young marriage
and I joined the chorus, howling the song of every lobo
that longs to be somewhere else. That's when I knew
I had to break loose from the pack
into the open spaces of the poem.

## Parrots

Parrots don't believe in evolution.
They squawk about the so-called missing links,

denying dino-tails with feathers have been found
in amber, cocksure that news of fossils

buried in the ground is fake. White wafers
on their tongues, they offer supplications

to their gods. They're into repetition,
have a reputation to protect. Hypocrites,

they hate pirates, desert islands, treasure
chests. Still show up for photo shoots

out of reverence for tradition — as long
as its for scale (times ten). They don't read

the newsprint on the bottoms of their cages,
just crap on the papers, eagle-eyeing

headlines to *Celebrity Skin* and *Hip Hop
Magazine*. They don't believe in global

warming — a hoax, they say, pointing
to recent freezes in Washington D.C.,

perched on bar stools lapping cocktails,
pink umbrellas hanging from their beaks,

while wives sit at home on the eggs. They swap
romantic partners after empty nests. Out of town

on business, they hit the kinky clubs, check out
swinging chicks in cages above their cherry heads.

Next morning, fly home in time for breakfast
with the kids, recounting tales of their trip —

plantains big as airplane wings,
crickets sweet as Krispy Kremes.

## Dear Frogs of Pinckneyville, Illinois

Forgive me for all the times I forced you
into Welch's Grape Jelly jars filled with cotton balls
soaked with ether from my father's starter fluid can

he sprayed into dead diesel engines
on frozen December mornings. I am truly sorry
for not throwing you higher. Please know that I wanted to

put you into orbit like Belka and Strelka, the first
warm-blooded animals to trick gravity and return
alive, but my nine-year old arm wasn't strong enough

to launch you over the peak of the barn's roof
crumbling into itself in the vacant lot next door.
I tried again and again as you tumbled behind glass

like green-clad daredevils in clothes dryers.
Naturally, I performed post-mortems, the point
of my mother's sewing scissors fitting perfectly

into openings seemingly created for entry. I squeezed
rough sides to lift white bellies, avoiding injury to organs
when I opened you up. You voiced no objections

when I showed the neighbor kids your digestive systems,
the contents of your stomachs, your kinked intestines —
totally in the interest of science. Like the other animals

slain so humans could travel safely to the moon.
I am sorry for them too. But not as much
as treating you as if you were created for us

to experiment on in order to protect those mothers' babies
who grew up to be astronauts. As if the empty womb
of space wasn't holy. As if you were not.

# Chicken

> *...beauty is nothing but the beginning of terror,*
> *which we still are just able to endure...*
> — Rilke

Aroma of hot lard, sweet meat buried beneath
pale, pimpled skin dredged in flour and herbs. The seething
iron skillet took both of my mother's blue-veined hands
to lift from the cracked burner cover. Drumsticks,
thighs, and breasts blooming into their golden moment
and then beyond — charred stipples of flesh sticking from neglect,
one at last with the black metal in a kind of victorious defeat,
a second death from which there is little to resurrect,
after a fight with my father. I remember
burnt blisters of hot corn on the cob, how the kernels burst
between my teeth, tiny suns gone nova. And was it heat
or salt that raised even smaller ones on my lips, pain
or pleasure, drawn so tightly across the flesh? Tight
as scales on the first snake, a tear in the corner
of Adam's eye, the beginning of manhood between
my legs, hair sprouting from the groin like silk
bursting through cornhusk whorls. As tight as teeth
clenched during first orgasm, the terror
I was — just — able to bear.

## Return of the Purple Martins

*Wichita Falls, TX, 1985*

A million feathers preen the evening sky, comb out
The yellow, gold and red strands, until black
Is a word for world, a tornadic pulsing
Thread, spooling back to the first
Nest of twigs as thin as tears
Or thoughts lost in the
Hollow-boned dance
Arcing toward the
Eye of the elm
Until the final
Purple martin
Spirals
In.
Until
The first
Purple martin
Spirals out of the
Eye of the elm, arcing
Toward the hollow-boned
Dance, lost in the thought of
Tears as thin as twigs, spooling
Forward to the next nest, a tornadic
Pulsing of yellow, gold and red threads
Until blue is a word for world, combing out
A million black feathers preening the morning sky.

## Horse Latitudes

You're driving I-10, somewhere between Las Cruces
and Deming. Feeling grounded. *All Things Considered*
on the radio, stories grazing the brown hills, voices
wet with static, licking at the sparse fence line
of automobile aerials moving west —
something about the legend of The Horse Latitudes,
the roiling vicissitudes of the Cape Horn Ocean
killing the wind, compelling sailors to throw horses
overboard to stay afloat — they found skeletons, necks
broken right next to sunken boats. In the same time frame,
the yellow stripe in the road turns
dark, widens and crosses over into your lane —
a streak of rust, then chestnut for miles. You can see it
beginning to turn again, this time coppery
in smell, and it's damp ahead — definitely
part of your brain says best slow down, says O
God! It's a roan in the road, lying on its side,
tied to the trailer behind a pickup truck,
hindquarters quivering. Quivering
in the blood-soaked arms of two men,
there are children crying, and a woman
is pulling a gun from the cab. As you swing wide,
one if its eyes, an unbroken egg full of white sky,
rolls back and flashes its lightning-red veins.
And in that moment you know everything
in the story is wrong — the ocean, the wind, the killing,
the men, all those horses at the bottom of the sea —
they jumped.

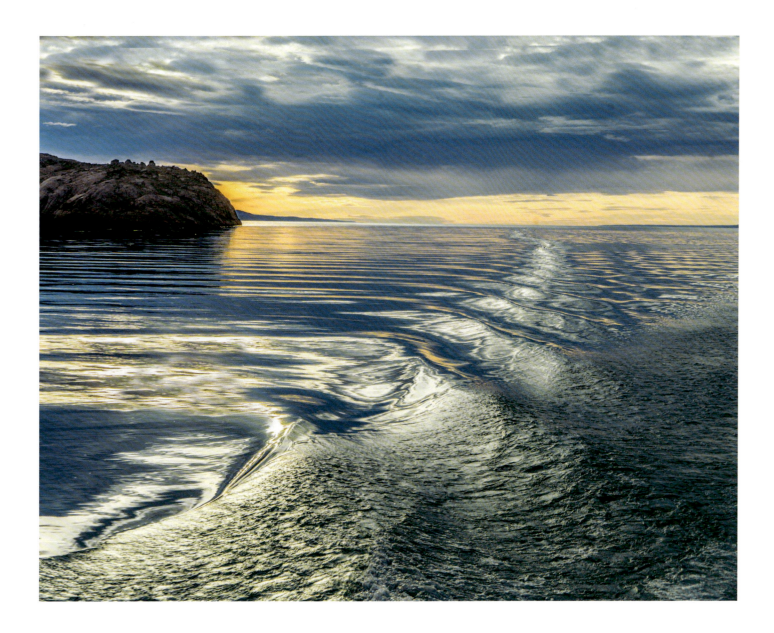

## Returning To My Childhood Home Thirty Years After Foreclosure

From across the street in my rental car,
the first thing I notice is the teardrop-
shaped juniper my father and I planted
when I was eight, grown taller now
than the roof, covering what was then
my bedroom window.
                              At the front door,
I ring the bell and mourn the loss of our brick
planter attached to the porch, the four o'clocks
sewn from brightly colored packets of magic,
seed mail-ordered from *Better Homes and Gardens*.
I touch the doorframe, wonder if it was the replacement
we had to buy, if I were the only boy that ever saw
his father walk through a door, splinter it
off its hinges.
                  I remember playing
on the living room rug, my mother yelling
in the kitchen at my father, her breaking into pieces
a burner cover on top of the stove, repeatedly
hammering exclamation points with an iron skillet,
screaming my father was never home, so she might as well
destroy every damned thing in the house.
                                        My father

always needing to prove himself better at destruction,
flung open all the cabinet doors, shattered our God-
damned golden wheat plates and bowls and mugs
against the wall.
                    When my mother threatened to call
the cops, my father went for his sawed-off shotgun,
dared her to dial the phone, loaded a single red shell
into the breach and clicked it shut.
                                  I covered my ears,
tracked my father's boot steps into the front hallway,
mother's muffled words trailing behind — little deaths
nipping at his scarred ears; marching into the front yard,
he filled the dark air with buckshot.
                              I can still hear the clack
as my mother locked the door behind him, the crack as he split it
in two walking back through it, the concussive sound of it
smacking the floor — "Don't ever try to lock me out again!"
Gathering his bags, he walked back through the emptiness
he had opened up in our house, loaded his truck
and gave himself back to the road.

                                      I ring the doorbell again.

Different notes sound from tones heard back then. Slight man
in shorts with coarse gray hair on his chest opens the door —
"Yes?" he says. "I grew up in this house, and was wondering
if I could come in for a minute or two…" I say.

                        I hear a woman's voice call from deep inside,
the rattle of a swamp cooler fan, the motor's whine; I feel a chill
of air as he shakes his head and shuts the door, leaving me outside,
standing with one foot on a stranger's porch, the other on what once was
a flowerbed — now dry unforgiving sand, runneled with long shadows.

## First Love

She was a sweet pickup — sixteen-year-old
Chevy truck — skirted-fenders, belly-dancer hips,
Windows curved around the cab, cupping
Private space like a bikini top. A little cramped
Inside, and the ride a bit rough,
But no real complaints. I covered her
Torn seat with blankets, padded the dash,
Painted the plastic lens of her dome light
Red, put an eight ball on the column shifter,
Where I'd rest my wrist after laying
Rubber in all three gears. O the ecstasy
From that bench seat night after night —
Star-blurred windshield, kaleidoscopic
Sun rising through fogged-up morning
Glass, a chapel with no confession booth,
Just the *kissing tone* from *Yours Truly,*
*KOMA, Oklahoma City* fading into a hiss —
Her turning over, moaning into life without a miss.

## Easy

as easy as
pi
lies next to random
numbers
you curl up beside me
sure that the curve of your legs will encircle
my straightness —
but never fully understanding our dance
no matter how many places
or how long
we try

Starbucks took you away: my barista, my double

tall, five-pump hazelnut, skinny, no-foam latte.
Now I sit alone in the basement of the Grand Food Mart

pouring axle-grease from a Bunn-O-Matic pot
into my Styrofoam cup: sugar, sugar —

only from The Archies. Black with no room
for cream. *Give it some time with the burner*

*on low, that flavor will turn into French roast —*
the clerk behind the counter offers

a Honey Bun or Hostess CupCake to cut the taste.
When she wants to splurge she takes a smoke break, opens up

a box of donut holes, sits down beside me — *Love,*
she begins, *is a many-splintered thing.*

## A Small Pebble

> *"Calculus," the branch of mathematics originally based on the summation of infinitesimal differences, is translated from the Latin as "a small pebble," like those used in an abacus.*

A redheaded young man in uniform
stares at a laminate menu, nervous
waitress waiting for him to decide between
coffee and tea. A calculus problem,

the solution to which will let him sit
in the corner booth until her shift ends.
Eyeing a four top by the door, ready
for their check, she senses a smaller tip
with each metronomic tic of fate's clock.

Coffee, black, he says. She tilts her Pyrex
pot toward his empty cup, reaches for the
bill of fare. He touches her hand, blurts out
a bold question. *Why?* she asks, withdrawing
her glass globe of burnt elixir. *Because...*
and he whispers something unexpected.

Now it's her turn to decide. And although
I'll not meet her for years, I have
much at stake in her decision —
will she agree to a first date, rushed
marriage a month after Pearl Harbor,
before he ships out for North Africa?

And when I tell you they are my parents,
you'll likely guess what she did, but not how
she turned away from the table, untied
her apron, chucked it at her boss,
along with her carbon-papered order pad,
walked past waiting customers to the porch,
picked a pebble from between two rough boards,
tossed it up, let it fall in her callused hand
like a loaded die, and threw it as hard
as she could at the newly-paved asphalt,
where it skipped a few times before it stuck
in the hot, dark tar, sank and disappeared,
becoming one with the road forever.

# Slow Dancing

In high school my mother forbade me to play
in dance band because swinging hips
to music was a sin. So instead I bugled
at Veterans of Foreign Wars funerals,

although at Green Lawn Cemetery, after twenty-one
shot salutes, I witnessed mourning bodies
swaying to ancient rhythms, holding partners close,
howling like lovers in need of release

as my trumpet sounded "Taps." The title
is said to come from the Dutch *taptoe*,
meaning close the beer taps and send the troops
home. A permission slip in the principal's office

signed by my mother allowed the post commander
of VFW 2182 to spring me from class an hour or two
before the service began. Al would call our house
the night before and I'd tell mom

I'd be burying the dead tomorrow afternoon.
The VFW Hall was a bar with a jukebox
and pool table. Al and his buddies played for money,
drank beer, and swapped yarns from two world wars,

while drunks dusted the dance floor to Benny Goodman's
licorice stick. As uniformed men loaded rifles and flags
into the van, I got to practice shots on the green felt.
Driving out to the cemetery, Al shook out a Sen-Sen

into my palm, reminded me not to tell mom
what went on down at the VFW Hall. It's okay,
I would tell him. I wasn't playing the music
they were dancing to — my transgressions venial.

A problem would only have arisen had she known
the mortal sins of mourners slow dancing to my horn.

## All roads

lead back to my mother swimming in black
humus, gumming the roots of the lupine

like an orchestra behind the curtain
tuning to concert A, the conductor

tapping his baton on the music stand, waiting
for the pull of bows across strings to settle

the score, free flags from seeds of notes rising
on the gorged page to wave in space above

the lines — the concave mirror of the bell
of my trumpet, its nickel-plated muzzle

on my lips, night after night, translucent bullets
of saliva dripping like white wine from a goblet

served on a tray of crushed thorns
that spill onto the stem of my arm

where the pain swerves to the shoulder
of the road that leads back to my mother.

# Acknowledgments

**Gary Topper:** When one asks oneself who is the most important person that made this book possible, for me it would be my husband, Tom Herington, whose pride, encouragement and passion for life all propelled me forward. Significantly, from the perspective of the art of photography, the Marin Photography Club and so many of its members, who are now good friends, gave to me the tools for perfecting my eye and abilities to produce the photographs presented in this book, and the many others that rest comfortably in my computer. And finally, the friendship and admiration of Terry's exquisite poems, brought together this collaboration of two living art forms.

**Terry Lucas** is grateful to the following journals, presses, anthologies, and websites where some of these poems first appeared, sometimes in slightly different versions.

*After Hours*: "Easy"
*Alaska Quarterly Review*: "Neighbors At 2 A.M."
*Banyan Review*: "By Any Other Name," "Morning Ritual," and "Safeway"
*Crosswinds*: "Parrots"
*Dactyls & Drakes*: "Dear Frogs of Pinckneyville, Illinois"
*Marin Poetry Center*: "First Love"
*Naugatuck River Review*: "A Small Pebble"
*Nostos*: "All Roads," "Good House Hunting," "Making Up the Dead," and
 "Starbucks took you away: my barista, my double"
*Open: Journal of Arts & Letters*: "Returning To My Childhood Home
 Thirty Years After Foreclosure"

"The Arrival," "Dharma Rain," "Infinity," "Horse Latitudes," "New Mexico Sighting," "Shiprock," "Recycling," "Return of the Purple Martins," "Spirit," "To the Fog," "The Thing Itself," and "Vortices" were all previously published in *Dharma Rain* (Saint Julian Press, 2016).

"By Any Other Name"
Some lines in the final two stanzas are reworked lines from "Corruption" by Srikanth Reddy.

"To the Fog" was the winner of the twelfth annual Littoral Press Broadside Contest, judged by Jaime Robles, letterpress printed in an edition of 55 at Littoral Press, Richmond, CA, Fall 2019.

"When She's Gone" appears in *If They Have Ears to Hear* (Southeast Missouri State University Press), winner of the 2012 Copperdome Chapbook Award.

"The Thing Itself"

This poem is a cento that borrows lines from the following poems and poets:

*The Thing Itself* is taken from the title of the poem "Not Ideas About the Thing But the Thing Itself" by Wallace Stevens.

*You know how hard it is sometimes just to walk in the streets / Downtown, how everything enters you* is line 1 from "Quantum," written by Kim Adonizio, published in *Tell Me*, BOA Editions, Ltd.: Rochester, 2000.

*Iron straight from the forge, fierce with tiny agitation* is line 1 from "Life Near 310 Kelvin," written by Greg Keith, published in *Life near 310 Kelvin*, SLG Books: Berkeley, Hong Kong, 1998.

*Rain ringing like teeth in the beggar's tin* is line 7 from "The City In Which I Love You," written by Li-Young Lee, published in *The City in Which I Love You*, BOA Editions, Ltd.: Brockport, New York, 1990.

*Like a sinking ship drowning its lights* is line 57 from *Altazor*, "Canto I, excerpt," written by Vincente Huidobro, published in *Poems for the Millennium, Vol. I*, University of California Press: London, 1995.

*Chalk beds   trilobites   giant ferns* is line 4 from "The Fetus' Curious Monologue," written by Amy Gerstler, published in *Ghost Girl*, Penguin Books: London, 2004.

*Whirr. The invisible sponsored again by white* is line 1 from "In The Hotel," written by Jorie Graham, published in *The Best American Poetry 1994*, Simon & Schuster: New York, 1994.

*Isotopes, pockets, dragonflies, bread* is lines 5 from "Crycek: The Confession," written by Susan Wheeler, published in *The American Poetry Review,* Vol. 28 / No. 2: March / April 1999.

*There is no Dictionary for this gathering* is line 93 from "Draft 55: Quiptych," written by Rachelle Blau DuPlessis, published in *The Best American Poetry 2004*, Scribner: New York, 2004.

*You might think you were Noah* is line 23 from "Nazareth By Rail," written by Matthew Niblock, published in *Scream When You Burn*, Incommunicado Press: San Diego, 1998.

*Failing to arrange a taxonomy of allergic substances* is line 21 from "Flower," written by Chris Gordon, published in *Scream When You Burn*, Incommunicado Press: San Diego, 1998.

*Our lives are like birds' lives, flying around blown away* is line 31 from "Drone and Ostinato," written by Charles Wright, published in *Negative Blue*, Farrar, Straus and Giroux: New York, 2000.

*Or some far horn repeating over water* is line 9 from "Nostalgia of the Lakefronts," written by Donald Justice, published in *The Best of the Best American Poetry*, Scribner: New York, 1998.

*Do we simply join our arcs* is from line 55 from "Midway," written by Gabriel Spera, published in *The Standing Wave*, Perennial (HarperCollins): New York, 2003.

*The way a seed is pressed into a hole* is line 11 from "Prayer," written by Kim Addonizio, published in *Tell Me*, BOA Editions, Ltd.: Rochester, 2000.

*Don't ask me any questions, I've seen how things* is line 18 from "1910 (Intermezzo)," written by Frederico Garcia Lorca, published in *Poet in New York*, Noonday Press: New York, 1994.

*Blink-quick or quicker still* is from line 2 of "Thinking," written by Matt Rader, published in *Grain Magazine*, Vol. 31, No. 2: Saskatchewan, 2003.

*Under the brown fog of a winter dawn* is line 61 of *The Waste Land*, "I. The Burial of the Dead," written by T.S. Elliot.

*Follow the light, the twist and drop of blackbirds from the tree* is line 9 from "So Here be my Harangue to God," written by Jim Nason, published by *Grain Magazine*, Vol. 30, No. 3: Saskatchewan, 2003.

Terry also wishes to thank the following people, without whom this book would be not possible or less than what it is: Tayve Neese and Jim Benton for their insightful comments on many poems in this collection; Lawrence Tjernell whose courage to take on this project has only been exceeded by his editorial and relational skills in guiding it to completion; to Gary Topper without whom these poems would still be seeking their relationship with one another and looking for a way to be fully realized in relationship to his work; and finally to Janet, for without her these poems and this book may never have been created, and if so, certainly not now, and not as well.

## The Collaboration

This book was born in the Sonoran Desert of Tucson over the 2018 Thanksgiving weekend. Gary Topper and Terry Lucas had many conversations about their individual passions, their personal visions of the world, and their different means of bringing those visions and passions to life. From these conversations came the idea of creating a mixed-genre work of Terry's poetry and Gary's photography that together would yield more than the mere sum. Gary and Terry began a collaboration that produced this book, an alliance of disparate backgrounds and approaches, a unity of words and images. But the process continues. They invite you, the reader and viewer, to become a part of the collaboration and to experience in your own creative way the elements and their union.

## About the Photographer

**Gary Topper**, a native Californian and an intrepid traveler, began his photographic journey in the 1960s eventually traveling to 65 countries where he photographed the people, places, and cultural events of the worlds he visited. His business career included the marketing of the wines of France, where he lived for 7 months, and of California, becoming the first wine marketer of the great wines of Napa and Sonoma. Upon retirement, he pursued his passion for photography as an art form. Recognition of his work includes Best of Show at the Marin County Fair, a one person show at the Throckmorton Gallery titled The Faces of Cuba, and many additional awards and group showings. Gary says of photography, "It is a medium that forces you to see the world rather than merely be in it. Capturing that moment in time — whether in color or monochrome — is a truly unique and exciting experience."

## About the Poet

**Terry Lucas** is the author of two previous full-length poetry collections: *Dharma Rain* (Saint Julian Press, 2016) and *In This Room* (CW Books, 2016). His two prize-winning chapbooks are *If They Have Ears to Hear* (Southeast Missouri State University Press, 2013), winner of the 2012 Copperdome Chapbook Award, and *Altar Call* (San Gabriel Valley Literary Festival, 2013). His poetry has appeared in numerous national journals, including *Alaska Quarterly Review*, *Best New Poets*, *Crab Orchard Review*, *Green Mountains Review*, and others. An excerpt of his memoir, *Flight*, was recently published in *Great River Review* (#66, 2019). Terry is Poet Laureate Emeritus of Marin County, California, a regular speaker at Dominican University of California's MFA Program, and a free-lance poetry coach. See www.terrylucas.com for more about him and his work.

## A Note on the Type

The text of this collection is set in Sabon, a serif typeface designed in the mid 1960s by Jan Tschichold. The face is based on the designs of Claude Garamond (1480 - 1561), an engraver and creator of some of the most beautiful and enduring typestyles in the world. The design of Sabon was released by Monotype, Linotype, and Stempel in 1967. The titles throughout this book have been set in Bollent, a very new face designed by Alfin Weniardi and released by the Fype Co. in 2020. It has been called "luxurious" and "elegant" with its variable baseline letterforms and calligraphic flair.

## Longship Press

Longship Press is an independent small-press publishing company located in San Rafael, California. It is the publisher of the literary journal *Nostos: Poetry, Fiction, and Art* and of several poetry collections. Calls for submissions to *Nostos* and solicitations for book manuscripts appear on its website, www.longshippress.com. The principal editor is Lawrence Tjernell.